The Middle Ages

MARY QUIGLEY

Heinemann Library
Chicago, Illinois

© 2003 Heinemann Library
a division of Reed Elsevier Inc.
Chicago, Illinois

Customer Service 888-454-2279

Visit our website at www.heinemannlibrary.com

Page layout by Mark Masseur
Map illustrations by John Fleck
Photo research by Amor Montes de Oca
Printed and bound in the United States by Lake Book Manufacturing, Inc.

07 06 05 04 03
10 9 8 7 6 5 4 3 2 1

Library of Congress Cataloging-in-Publication Data
The Middle Ages / Mary Quigley.
        p. cm. -- (Understanding people in the past)
Summary: Presents an overview of culture and society during the Middle Ages.
Includes bibliographical references and index.
  ISBN 1-4034-0387-2 (HC), 1-4034-0607-3 (Pbk.)
  1. Middle Ages--Juvenile literature. 2. Civilization, Medieval--Juvenile literature. [1. Middle Ages. 2. Civilization, Medieval.] I. Series.
      D117 .M5 2002
    909.07--dc21

                    2002002347

Acknowledgments
The author and publisher are grateful to the following for permission to reproduce copyright material:
Title page, p. 51T Elio Ciol/Corbis; pp. 5, 6T, 7B, 8, 11, 13, 14T, 15, 17, 20, 25T, 27, 32, 35, 38, 39T, 42, 43, 44, 45, 52, 53, 54, 55, 57 The Granger Collection; pp. 6B, 9, 10, 12T, 14B, 18, 21, 26, 28, 33, 34T, 40, 47 North Wind Pictures; p. 7T Ric Ergenbright/Corbis; pp. 12B, 16, 24, 25B, 41 Archivo Iconografico, S. A./Corbis; p. 19 Leonardo de Selva/Corbis; pp. 22, 30, 58 Gianni Dagli Orti/Corbis; p. 23 Historical Picture Archive/Corbis; pp. 29, 51B, 59 Scala/Art Resource; pp. 31, 39B, 48 The Bridgeman Art Library, New York; p. 34B Corbis; p. 36 Museo de Arte Antiga Lisbon/The Art Archive; p. 37 Angelo Hornak/Corbis; p. 46 Historical Picture Archive/Corbis; p. 49 Snark/Art Resource; p. 50T Araldo de Luca/Corbis; p. 56 British Library/The Art Archive

Cover photograph: The Granger Collection

Some words are shown in bold, **like this.** You can find out what they mean by looking in the glossary.

Contents

People in the Middle Ages

The Roman Empire

The Middle Ages is the name for approximately 1,000 years between the collapse of the **Roman Empire** in 476 C.E. and the famous journey that Christopher Columbus made across the Atlantic Ocean in 1492 C.E. Historians call this the Middle Ages because it came between classic Greek and Roman civilizations, and our modern history. We refer to events and things of the Middle Ages as **medieval.**

The Roman Empire was very large. After its collapse, many smaller empires throughout Europe emerged.

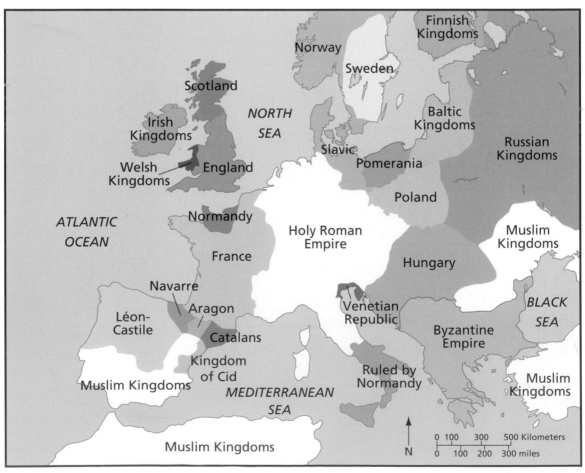

The Roman Empire was a vast territory with a complicated government, large cities, beautiful art, and many famous scholars. But, the Roman Empire could not survive its many problems. Poor leadership, a failing economy, invasions, and corruption among the people led to its decline. After its collapse, a time began when empires would be smaller and there would be struggles and disputes about leadership.

In the feudal system, everyone had a specific role in society.

The eastern part of the Roman Empire survived long after the western part collapsed. But from 476 C.E. on, instead of being part of a huge and powerful empire, people would find themselves living under the leadership of local rulers. These rulers struggled to keep control of their kingdoms.

The feudal system

As Europe divided into smaller kingdoms, the people created a new type of government. The **feudal system** developed as a way to manage large kingdoms. The many rulers placed **lords,** or landlords, in charge of large areas of land. The feudal system was agrarian—it was designed for societies where most of the people were farmers. Farmers who were free were called peasants.

Better than slavery?

Landlords had **serfs** work the land in exchange for food and a place to live. While the life of a serf was hard, it was somewhat better than slavery—a common practice in the Roman Empire. Lords needed to have large numbers of serfs to maintain the land, raise crops and livestock, and sometimes defend the **castles** where they lived.

How Do We Know?

Written records

Written records tell us much about the Middle Ages. An example of this is *The Canterbury Tales* by Geoffrey Chaucer. Chaucer wrote a set of stories that he imagined were told by people on a **pilgrimage.** His pilgrims were going to visit the shrine of Saint Thomas à Becket. Chaucer wrote in the latter part of the Middle Ages, though he is also considered an early **Renaissance** poet.

Historians also study written records that have been found or handed down through families. People who lived in **castles** often kept a record of their purchases, menus, and other household

Literature, such as Chaucer's *The Canterbury Tales*, helps us know more about how people lived in the Middle Ages.

St. Thomas à Becket was killed by four knights because he had angered King Henry II. He disagreed with the king about how **clergy,** found guilty of crimes in Church courts, should be punished. The knights overheard Henry II say that he wished he could be rid of Becket. They thought this meant that the King would be pleased if they killed him.

A church was an important place for people in medieval villages and towns.

details. These records contain a lot of interesting information about what people ate, how they entertained, and who the important people of the time were.

Buildings and artifacts

Some castles and churches from the Middle Ages are still standing. Everyday objects, tools, armor, and artwork have lasted through the years and tell us many things about the materials people used. These objects also tell us about their craft-making skills. Artifacts tell us about how people lived and what they thought was important. Artifacts also give us information about **medieval** people's work, their play, and their religious beliefs.

Tools from the Middle Ages tell us much about the type of work people did then.

Tapestries

Tapestries are beautifully woven fabrics that are like a painting made of fibers. They portrayed saints and heroes and sometimes everyday life. Tapestries were beautiful and practical because they could be hung on the cold walls of a **castle** to make it warmer. Only the very wealthy could afford tapestries. They would often take them along on journeys or when they moved to a new castle. Tapestries became treasured heirlooms that were handed down within families. Some tapestries can be seen in museums today. They can tell us about what people thought during the Middle Ages.

Tapestries were beautiful and useful art. Hung on the castle walls, they helped make life in a cold castle a little more comfortable. Some tapestries were only used to tell a story, like the Bayeaux Tapestry below.

Manuscripts

In the Middle Ages, books were very expensive and very few existed compared to after the **printing press** was invented in the **Renaissance.** During the Middle Ages, books were made by hand. These books are usually called manuscripts. Each page was copied carefully with beautiful letters and illustrations. This process is called illumination. Professional illuminators would use layers of paint, careful sketching, and sometimes **gold leaf** to embellish lettering and add illustrations.

Manuscripts, such as this one, had illustrated pages. Sometimes the pages had gold leaf on them. Every page was a work of art. The cover might be decorated with jewels.

Reading and writing

In much of Europe, most people could not read or write. People did not learn to read and write because books were scarce and few people went to school. Reading and writing were not necessary skills for the average person. Stories were handed down orally and agreements were verbal. One exception was the **clergy.** They encouraged reading and writing. Because of their knowledge of written language, they were considered by the general public to have a great gift from God. **Monks** used their knowledge to create many of the manuscripts of the Middle Ages.

Kings and Nobles

In the **feudal system,** everyone had a certain place in society. Each person's place in society determined how much influence and money they had. It was usually very difficult to change from one place in society to another. Kings, queens, and their children were at the top.

Kings usually came to power by being the oldest son of the previous king—they inherited the throne. But, an eldest son who seemed unqualified for the job could be passed over in favor of another son or even an uncle that the **nobles** thought would be a better king. Sometimes, people believed that a king was chosen by God.

King Henry VI and the Queen receive a book from John Talbot, Earl of Shrewsbury. They are surrounded by members of their court.

Nobles enjoyed many rewards from their allegiance to royalty, like land and privilege.

Queens were often the wives of kings. Sometimes the throne was inherited by a daughter. When this happened, her husband, if she had one, could be the king if the people felt he was capable. Sometimes kingships were disputed and there were efforts to overthrow leaders.

Nobles

Nobles might be called Duke, Earl, or Baron. Nobles received their status from **family lineage.** Nobles were the ruling class at a local level. They would join forces with kings and queens to create **alliances** and larger kingdoms.

Lords and Knights

Lords

A **lord** was granted his role by the king or by inheritance. A lord, or landlord, was a wealthy and prominent person who used **serfs** to work his land in exchange for having some protection and basic needs met. A lord also served as a judge. He had to travel a lot to collect rents from the serfs, or possibly from renting peasants who worked the land he oversaw. Rents may have been paid in goods and crops, not just money.

The lord of a castle was responsible for making sure that the peasants fulfilled their agreements.

Becoming a knight

A knight began his training as a page when he was eight years old. As a teenager, he would become a squire. To be dubbed a

Armor was first made of chainmail. Chainmail is connected links of metal. Knights sometimes wore light cloth tunics over their armor to keep the metal from becoming hot in the sun.

knight, a young man had to go through training, obtain a suit of armor, and sometimes even perform certain ceremonies.

A loyal knight might have a **castle.** In exchange, he would be a landlord and also a soldier in times of war. He might go to war himself, but often would hire someone to go in his place. Going to war himself would mean leaving his family, home, and work.

Practice

A **melee** was for group practice. In a melee, knights practiced their warrior skills in a mock battle. Individuals competed against each other in jousts. A joust is like a melee except that it is done with two knights charging individually at each other. Gradually, practice battles were replaced with more theatrical, staged performances.

The art of creating coats of arms is called heraldry. There were strict rules about it. Each design had a color and silver or gold. There might be an animal and sometimes another symbol like a cross.

Coats of arms

Coats of arms were placed on knights' shields. This was very important because when knights were in their armor, it was nearly impossible to tell who was friend and who was foe. So, the shield told on which side the knight was fighting. It also gave important information about the knight's **family lineage** and social rank.

Coats of arms, or crests, were used in other ways as well. **Nobles** used them as official **seals** and **merchants** and craftworkers used them to represent their trade or craft.

Religion

Religion was an important part of people's lives. After the fall of the **Roman Empire,** western Europe was not unified by a government. Instead, the Catholic Church was the only unifying institution left. The laws of the Church created a certain amount of order in an otherwise chaotic time. The Church was also a source of comfort in a time of **plagues,** war, and poverty for much of the population. Almost everyone, no matter what their social class, went to church on Sundays and holy days. The Catholic Church was as powerful as any royal family.

Saints

Catholics loved the saints and tried to learn from their example how to live better lives. Catholics also believed that saints could help them in times of trouble, if their aid was requested in a prayer.

Power

Until the end of the Middle Ages, the majority of people in western Europe were Catholic. Although there was not one big government, the Church provided some amount of connection and communication between regions. Because of its power and

Martin Luther challenged some of the ideas of the Catholic Church.

The Catholic Church was very powerful in the Middle Ages.

influence, the Catholic Church obtained much money in the form of **tithes.**

Members of the Church

Most people followed the rules of the Catholic Church, which included a leader, called a pope; various **clergy** such as priests, friars, and nuns; and all the members. Nearly every small village had a church and a priest. Often the priest was the only person who could read and write in the village. The only formal education available during the Middle Ages was through the Church.

Illuminated manuscripts were copied by hand in monasteries and convents. It could take anywhere from months to years to produce a single book.

Other religions

Early in the Middle Ages, Jewish **merchant** towns were valued for **trade** and finance. These towns served as places where imported items such as perfume, spice, silk, and jewels were exchanged for western European furs, swords, lumber, and slaves. Jews tended to live in their own communities and married within their own faith. Throughout the Middle Ages, people of other faiths tried to drive the Jews out of their communities and even committed violence against them for not accepting the same religious beliefs.

During the Middle Ages, Islam was growing rapidly in the Middle East and began to find followers in other areas as well. Some western Europeans were Muslims. A group of Muslims called the Moors ruled in southern Spain for about 250 years during the Middle Ages. Sometimes people of other religions hated or feared the Muslims. Like the Jews, they were often persecuted. But by the end of the Middle Ages, many western Europeans had become interested in the wealth and knowledge of the Muslims.

Monasteries, Churches, and Cathedrals

Monasteries were places where **clergy** could study quietly and pray. Lay brothers—clergy yet to be **ordained**—did the fieldwork, like tending the grounds and gardens. **Monks** lived at the monastery. **Cloisters** were built with study compartments along the side. Two meals were eaten each day. The warming house, kitchen, and hospital were the only areas with a fire.

Female clergy lived in convents. Convents were simple, quiet places for prayer, like monasteries. Their role was probably to support the parish priest. They might have also educated children and cared for the sick.

Every village had at least a simple church with a parish priest. In the Middle Ages,

A monastery was a humble residence for monks. Worship and study occupied their day until well after sunset. This monk is giving a cross to a knight leaving for a **crusade.**

Cities took great pride in having beautiful cathedrals. Canterbury Cathedral in England was built in the late sixth century. It became a **pilgrimage** site for many during the Middle Ages after the murder of Archbishop Thomas à Becket in 1170.

people did not travel far from home. They generally went only to church, the nearby **castle,** or a shop if one was close.

Cathedrals

Larger towns or cities had cathedrals. Towns would compete over which had the most beautiful cathedral. Many windows were made of stained glass. Art, such as sculptures, paintings, and woodwork, decorated the interior. In the latter part of the Middle Ages, the Catholic Church became a **patron** of the arts—employing the best artists to create murals, sculptures, and castings to portray biblical events.

Noble poverty

Serfs of the Middle Ages found joy and comfort in family, friends, home, and church. They even believed that their poverty was noble and would be rewarded in heaven. Peasants paid a tenth of their grain as a **tithe** to the priest of their village.

Crusades

During the Middle Ages, there were **crusades.** Groups of people led by religious figures went into battle against people who were not Christian. Their primary goal was to drive out or convert people who did not share the Christian belief. Christianity is based on peaceful beliefs. But those who joined the crusades showed a very violent side.

To unite Europe

Christians also were motivated by factors aside from religious beliefs. Some crusade leaders thought that a successful crusade would unite the people of Europe. It would bring a return to life as it was during the

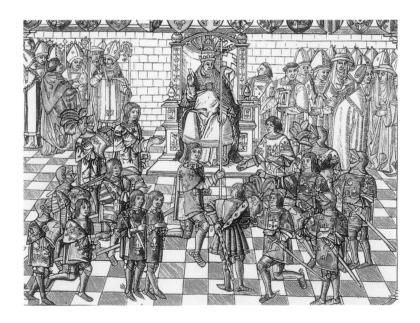

The crusades were battles fought because of religious differences. Crusaders usually fought against anyone who was not Christian. The first crusade was called by Pope Urban II in 1095.

Peter the Hermit was a traveling **evangelist** who led the Peasant's Crusade. A crowd of farmers and **artisans** joined with him for the adventure of going on a crusade. They reached **Constantinople** in 1096, where a displeased emperor handed them over to the **Turks**.

Roman Empire—a large nation bound together with a common set of laws. It could reduce local wars and promote **trade**. Instead, the crusades brought much suffering to religious groups like Judaism and Islam. The crusades also harmed the reputation of Christians as a peaceful people.

Aftermath of the crusades

Eventually, crusaders began to see that their opponents were not the terrible people that they had imagined. Their contact with them led to some amount of understanding. To this day, people are still trying to mend the divisions that were caused by the crusades.

Family Life

In the Middle Ages, women primarily worked at home—sewing, cooking, mending, watching the fire, and tending the children. When men who lived in **castles** were away, their wives often took charge. **Lords** traveled frequently. During those times, the lady of the house managed the meals, accounts, and businesses.

Women took charge when necessary. They guarded the castle, led the defense if the castle came under siege, and entertained influential guests.

Marriage

Girls were usually married when they were about fourteen years old. Men married at various ages. A man might delay marriage until after studying at a university or until after becoming a knight. A man might also delay marriage for lack of money. It was common for older men to marry younger women, partly because they had lost a previous wife or wives during childbirth—a somewhat risky event during the Middle Ages. Upon marriage, women gave their husbands a sum of money known as a "marriage portion." In turn, she was entitled to one-third of her husband's wealth.

Marriages were often arranged. Children as young as seven years old might be promised to another. A marriage joined the political and business interests of both families together.

Sometimes women resisted tradition and married for love. Women who were widows often remained unmarried if they had the financial means to survive.

Children

Children were usually born at home. If their home was in a rural area, the father assisted the mother with delivery. In towns and villages, neighbors, other family members, or even a passing stranger might be summoned for help. Just like today, opinions on raising children varied. Some people thought they were basically good and that because of their innocence they could be wiser than adults. Other people thought children were wild and unruly and needed strict discipline and religious study.

The wealthy had one or more **midwives** who were experienced with delivering babies. There were hospitals, but they were more like places of refuge for the poor, widowed, and sick.

Medieval Clothing

In the early Middle Ages, clothes were made from local materials like wool, animal skins, and **flax.** Linen was made by softening the stems of the flax plant. The strong flax fibers were spun into linen cloth. Women also turned wool into yarn. Women could spin wool while they were tending children or traveling. Women in poor families wove their own clothing and blankets.

Peasants wore clothes made from durable fabrics to fit their working lifestyle.

Everyday clothes

Peasant or **serf** men and boys wore tunics made of wool and loose pants called breeches. Sometimes, they wore long stockings or wrapped their legs with long strips of cloth. Over their tunics they wore a sleeveless cape called a surcoat. Women wore a longer tunic that looked like a loose dress. Sometimes they wore a hood with a veil that draped across the throat.

Clothes for the wealthy

As **trade** and travel increased, luxury fabrics such as silk, **damask**, and velvet became available. The wealthy dressed in beautiful, colorful clothes. Peasants generally continued to use coarse fabrics. **Nobles** were the only ones allowed to wear certain styles of

People in the Middle Ages cared a lot about how they looked and smelled. They enjoyed perfumes and baths.

clothing. Clothing made it clear who was rich and who was poor. Hats and jewelry were popular fashion items.

Makeup

In addition to fashion, women of the Middle Ages had an interest in makeup, too. Pale complexions or rouged cheeks were achieved using makeup that was sold by traveling peddlers or town **merchants.** Often the ingredients were irritating and sometimes poisonous!

Wealthy men wore variations on the tunic, but with decorations and colorful leggings. Wealthy women often had dresses with detachable sleeves that allowed them to reuse the main part of the dress. Children from wealthy homes usually dressed like miniature adults.

Growing Up and Going to School

Children played games like leap frog, tug-of-war, and ball games. Chess and backgammon were also played. Children shared tales about everyday life, legends, and biblical stories. They were expected to do chores and help take care of the household and siblings or aging relatives. Some children were sent away at a young age to learn a skill or live with a relative. So, siblings often did not spend their childhood together.

Children sometimes worked in a **lord's** manor. Boys might take care of the horses. Girls would work in the kitchen. Many people died before age 30 because there were many serious diseases during the Middle Ages. Also, many died in childbirth. Teenagers were considered adults since life expectancy was shorter.

Like today, **medieval** children enjoyed playing games.

Children were expected to do their share of the work. Peasant children helped with the farm chores. Here, children help take care of hunting dogs.

Boys

Until about 1200, most children did not go to school. Only boys who would become church leaders or the children of royalty and **nobles** received formal schooling. The rest of the boys learned fieldwork or got an **apprenticeship** with a blacksmith, potter, shoemaker, hatmaker, tailor, clothworker, dyer, or other skilled craftworker.

Girls

Most girls did not go to school. A few received some education at convents. Girls were expected to learn housekeeping skills, manners, and how to be a good wife and mother.

Only some children received a formal education during the Middle Ages.

Many young boys learned a skill from a craftworker instead of going to school.

The Farming Year

Farming was primarily done by peasants, **serfs,** and the people who lived at monasteries. They grew wheat, oats, hay, turnips, and other vegetables. They worked long days. The type of work they did depended on the season. Preparing the land for crops, planting seeds, weeding, and harvesting created a yearly cycle for those who farmed.

The **feudal system** depended greatly on serfs. Serfs were the ones who did the farm work necessary for a feudal society to succeed.

Farmers raised animals such as sheep, cows, chickens, and ducks for their eggs and milk. Meat was not a large part of the **medieval** diet. An ongoing supply of milk and eggs was more valuable than a brief feast of meat from the same animal.

Since serfs were farming land that belonged to a **lord**, there were many restrictions. Serfs had to pay to have their grains milled at the lord's mill. The flour was taken to the baker to be turned into bread. Serfs could not use their own mill. If they tried to and were caught, then they had to pay a fine and their mill would be destroyed.

Wool

In addition to crops, livestock was important. Wool **trade** was profitable in the Middle Ages. Monasteries were even involved in this trade, raising sheep on their land for wool.

Serfs and Peasants

The **feudal system** depended upon the loyalty and hard work of **serfs** and peasants. Serfs agreed to work the land of a **lord** in exchange for protection in times of war, shelter, and a share of the crops. Peasants were free, but poor farmers. The vast majority of people living in the Middle Ages were peasants or serfs. They far outnumbered all the other social classes combined.

These workers are receiving orders from their lord before going to work in the fields.

Most of the food a serf grew went to the lord of the manor. They could not hunt or fish on the lord's land without permission. Nor would there be much land available to a peasant that was free to hunt. The lord's land might stretch as far as the peasant would travel. Serfs were "bound to the land," meaning that when the land was sold, they came under the authority of the new owner. They could only gather firewood if they paid a fee called a "wood penny," and they could only have fallen branches.

Peasants found happiness and comfort from family and the Church. The Church gave them confidence that their hard work and good deeds would be rewarded.

Medicine and Healing

Doctors

There were doctors in the Middle Ages, but they were still trying to figure out how the human body worked. They thought the body was made up of fluids called **humors,** and that illness was caused when one was out of balance. Their understanding of anatomy was largely based on the work of Galen, a doctor who lived a few hundred years before the Middle Ages.

Highly qualified doctors were often well paid and traveled from royal court to royal court. The wealthy might have their own paid physician on staff. People had to be careful, though. Sometimes people pretending to be doctors would travel around getting money for cures that would not work or that were dangerous. There is some evidence of women being licensed to practice medicine.

Medicine and the Church

In northern Europe, medicine was practiced and regulated by the Church. Illness was seen as punishment from God. Illness would be treated with prayer or by asking for a saint's help. Folk remedies, such as herbal medicine, were also used.

Medieval doctors used both traditional and new methods to cure illness. This doctor (left) is taking the pulse of a young student.

Medical advances

Throughout the late Middle Ages, new medical techniques emerged. Grafts of skin and bones were used to repair facial or other injuries. Antiseptic surgery was invented in the late Middle Ages. This meant that great care was used in keeping everything that came in contact with the patient free of germs. Some medical practices from the Greeks and Romans had also been handed down to the people of the Middle Ages.

Medieval doctors tasted urine to diagnose sugar level. Doctor-prescribed remedies during the Middle Ages might include making a religious **pilgrimage,** having a massage, or using herbal cures.

Some new, some old

Many features of modern medicine emerged at this time. The hospital was invented in the Middle Ages. Doctors went to medical school at universities and they were licensed to practice medicine. However, many of the people who took care of the sick were still using folk remedies. People who did not live near cities that had universities had to rely upon whatever methods or cures were available to them.

Herbs were used as natural remedies for many illnesses. Dill was thought to help with digestion and was believed to ward off evil spells. Mint was claimed to cure over 40 illnesses, including poor memory and headaches. **Hyssop** was used as a laxative and **fennel** revived anyone who felt faint.

A Medieval City

Roman roots

Medieval cities were generally built among the ruins of the **Roman Empire.** Many of the buildings from that time survived and people remained in certain cities. The geographic features that had attracted people to settling in certain areas in ancient times, still held true in medieval times. Cities formed in spots that still had good waterways, or a nice hill to place a **castle** upon, or in an area that had varied game. The collapse of the Roman Empire had brought some destruction and decay to the cities. However, by the end of the Middle Ages,

Medieval cities showed a resemblance to classic Greece and Rome. This is a cross-section of Filippo Brunelleschi's design for the dome of Santa Maria del Fiore Cathedral in Florence, Italy.

Trade was primarily local in the Middle Ages—**merchants** sold what was readily available to them. These shops line a street in medieval France.

people were rebuilding and learning to imitate the styles of classic Roman and Greek art and **architecture.**

Center of trade

Medieval cities thrived on **trade.** For most of the Middle Ages, this trade was mainly local. By the end of the Middle Ages, trade was more far-reaching. Explorers were creating new trade routes to other western European countries, eastern Europe, and the Mediterranean. The goods of other regions were becoming well-known in western Europe. Cities became busy centers for exchanging goods, ideas, and culture. People slowly became aware of the world beyond their own town, city, or village.

Town and Village

Roads

Many people lived in small, rural villages. The main road led to the manor and to the nearest church. Roads were narrow and there were no streetlights. It was usually dark by the time the day's work was done, so people had to carry lanterns to travel after sunset.

Why leave?

Cities and towns were a cluster of homes and shops near the **castle** and often within a fortified wall. Cities, villages, and towns were self-sufficient for most of the Middle

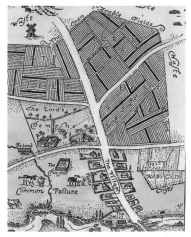

Villages were communities in the countryside.

Towns and cities grew near the protection of a castle. This **medieval** port town lies within a protective wall.

Ages. People could live their whole life without traveling beyond the borders of their city, town, or village, depending upon where they lived.

Castles as protection

Cities, towns, and villages grew up around castles. In times of siege, people would seek protection at the castle. While villages were spread out beyond the castle walls in rural areas, towns or cities grew up inside the walls. When villagers fled attack, they would set their village on fire to make sure the enemy didn't get any food or weapons.

A castle was a refuge for those under protection of a **lord** in times of war. Here, women and children flee a sacked town.

Medieval Homes

Common homes

Most homes had a table, benches, beds, chests, and stools made of wood. Houses were made of wood with a thatch roof. There was one downstairs room with a hearth for cooking and heating. A big wooden table in front of the hearth was used for dining. A ladder led upstairs where there were small rooms for sleeping.

Mighty castles

Castles belonged to **lords,** who might be barons, bishops, or **nobles.** Castles had towers so the lord could view his land from safety. A castle was both a home and a fort. A strong stone wall surrounded the houses and shops of the town near the castle.

In the Middle Ages, a peasant's home was simple and uncluttered.

In the White Tower, which is part of the Tower of London, medieval kings lived here with their families and their court in the top story. The government used the floor below.

There was very little privacy in castles. The wealthy had some sort of bed and the guests would sleep on the floor or on a simple mat or cot with the dogs. Boats were brought along waterways that ran alongside the castle.

Life in a castle

Inside a castle there was an entire community. Here are just a few of the jobs that people did to keep a castle going:

- stable grooms looked after the horses;
- a treasurer and a steward helped the lord collect rents in the form of cash or crops;
- jesters and minstrels provided entertainment;
- the cook had an entire staff to help him carry and serve the food to the guests;
- a spinster made thread so the weaver could make cloth;
- a laundress washed the clothes;
- knights and squires prepared for warfare;
- the falconer trained hawks to catch rabbits and game birds; and
- dog keepers gave careful attention to the hunting dogs.

Cooking and Eating

Meals at a castle

At a **castle,** the **lord,** his family, and guests had chairs at meals. Everyone else had benches. Breakfast was a small snack after church mass. The lord, his family, and guests might have white bread with cold meat or cheese and wine. Dinner, between 10 A.M. and noon, was the biggest meal of the day. Cups were made of silver, **pewter,** wood, or horn. Spoons were provided, but guests brought their own knives. Forks didn't show up until near the end of the Middle Ages. Silver platters were used to serve food to

The wealthy had spectacular feasts.

A young family member might say the blessings at a **merchant** family's meal. Merchants ate smaller meals with fewer **retainers**. Generally, there was one large meal around noon and a smaller snack or meal during the morning and evening.

the **nobles.** Wood platters were used for everyone else. Instead of plates, a trencher of dry bread, either fashioned as a slab or a bowl, was used. The trencher was not eaten, but saved to give to the poor. Supper at the castle was a light meal at sunset. Several small side dishes and cheese were served.

Peasants

Peasants and **serfs** ate humble meals of porridge, turnips, dark bread, and beer or ale. They might have had a salad of parsley, mint, garlic, thyme, and rosemary, with a vinegar or **verjuice** dressing. During hog slaughter season they might have had pork or bacon. They generally ate fish instead of other meats.

A peasant might have had trouble finding enough food for his livestock. Peasants and serfs were sometimes given permission by their lord to knock acorns out of trees for their pigs to eat. This was helpful in the fall when other food was scarce.

Feasting and Fasting

A medieval feast

Eating was a favorite **medieval** activity and an opportunity for socializing. A medieval feast had a dazzling buffet of food. Animal heads were left on, or put back on, after cooking. Swans were served covered in **gold leaf.** Feathers were put back on after cooking, and before serving.

Fruits of the Middle Ages were small and mostly grew in the wild. People thought they were unwholesome and seldom served fruit. However, at a feast there might be apples, plums, pears, peaches, and nuts. Spices were

People during the Middle Ages thought that animals served at banquets should still look like animals. So, they put things like feathers back on after cooking and added decorations such as gold leaf.

used to cover the taste of spoiling food. Specialty foods at feasts included sugars flavored with rose and violet, dandelion wine, and jelly.

Trenchers were stale bread upon which stews were served. They were saved after a meal to give to the poor to eat.

Fasting and sharing

Despite the medieval love of food, religious restrictions required that people **fast** at certain times. In addition, the religious belief of charity meant that people had to share food with the poor. Sharing with the poor would benefit the community in many ways, such as keeping the poor from rising up against the **nobles** and promoting public health. Sometimes, the unpredictable events of nature ruined crops. Crop failure brought cycles of famine to the poor, who mostly relied on what they could grow themselves.

Sports and Recreation

Hunting

Hunting was both a way of providing food and a way of practicing for war. **Wild boar** was hunted with the help of dogs. Kennel boys were employed to feed the dogs, care for them when they were sick, pull thorns from their paws, patch them up after a hunt, and take them for runs. Deer, wolf, and brown bear were also hunted with the help of dogs. Hunting with crossbows allowed both men and women to practice their archery skills. When not hunting with crossbows, people hunted with swords, knives, and spears.

Hunting had many purposes. It provided food, recreation, and practice for battle for the people who participated.

Using falcons and other birds of prey to catch small game was a popular sport in the Middle Ages.

Falconry

Falconry was a popular sport. A **lord** would carry his falcon on his left wrist. He had to wear a thick leather glove to keep the falcon's talons from scratching him. At his command, the falcon would fly off to capture a bird. Women flew smaller birds, such as merlins. When a lord did business in the great hall, he would often have his falcon tethered to his finger on a silk string called a jess. Bells on a falcon's legs helped the falconer to find the bird.

Games and fun

When not working, people played board games and cards. Chess was also popular. In the Middle Ages, people were entertained by jugglers and **acrobats.** Others played music and sang. They went to jousts and **melees** to watch knights practice.

Manners

At the table

Just like today, there were rules for behavior at the dinner table in **medieval** times. Here are just a few of the things people were not allowed to do at the table:

- gnaw on bones with their teeth;
- poke their fingers in eggs;
- spit across the table;
- wipe their mouths on their sleeves;
- bite into the trencher;
- put elbows on the table;
- slurp soup or belch;
- wipe teeth or a knife on the tablecloth;
- butter bread with thumbs; or
- feed dogs scraps from the table.

Despite a lot of mealtime rules, eating in the Middle Ages could be quite a mess. Even though it was considered bad manners, a man in this illustration is feeding a dog from the table.

Code of chivalry

The code of **chivalry**, which was adopted to subdue the violence of knighthood, called for virtue and charity. Knights were expected to care for the sick, oppressed, and elderly. This knightly code spilled over into the rest of Middle Age culture.

Manners were also influenced by the teachings of Christianity. People applied biblical virtues to their dealings with others. As is often the case in history, people did not always live up to their own high standards. The code of chivalry was created in response to efforts by the Church to reduce the violent nature of knights. This overlapping of manners and Christian morals was a key feature of the Middle Ages.

The code of chivalry set rules that affected all of **feudal society**, even though it was originally intended for knights.

Crafts and Craftworkers

Craftworkers made jugs and bowls out of clay, folding chairs, and jewelry boxes with strong locks. **Pewter** was poured into molds to make jugs and dishes. It was known as the "poor man's silver" because it was cheap. Blacksmiths made tools, weapons, and cooking utensils from iron.

Mosaics were a popular form of art in the Middle Ages. Italian **frescoes** were painted into wet plaster. Candlemakers, jewelers, and glovemakers worked from their shops in town. Leather workers, potters, and others who needed lots of space to work settled near the edge of town.

Fine glass and silver were made in France and Venice. Explorers obtained gold crafts in the Americas, melted them down, and molded them into blocks to be shipped back to Europe.

Guilds

Craftworkers and **artisans** wanted to make sure that only quality goods were sold, in order to maintain the reputation of their craft. To ensure a high standard of crafts and to keep the **trade** of goods on fair ground,

Wood

Wood was used to make boats, carts, and furniture such as benches, tables, and chests. **Nobles** decorated the walls of their homes with wooden panels. In France and Scotland, craftworkers painted pictures on wooden ceiling panels using bright colors.

Medieval craftworkers were often artists as well. These are just some of the goods created during this time.

Each guild was identified by an emblem. The emblem might reflect an aspect of the craft or service, or a patron saint.

they created guilds. To sell certain items, a person had to belong to the appropriate guild. Each guild was for a certain craft. In this way, there would be no competition from cheap, imitation goods. Also, the valuable skills of the craftworkers were handed down to people who needed to learn the required methods.

Guilds offered **apprenticeships.** They had requirements for training and skill levels, so the only people who could claim to be in the guild had to meet certain standards. People looking for a certain good or service would generally select from the guilds. This prevented the unskilled workers—who offered cheaper, inferior products—from developing a customer base.

Travel and Transportation

The Middle Ages was a time when people rarely traveled beyond their own town or village. The town or village was self-sufficient, so it was not necessary to leave for **trade** goods. Also, while there was a well-developed system of roads during the **Roman Empire**, its collapse left no one to oversee it. Government was very localized and kings and **lords** did not bother with things outside their borders.

Why travel?

Travelers faced bad roads or no roads. They also faced the problems of robbery and kidnappings that could happen when a person got too far beyond the safety of their own town or village. **Serfs** were not permitted to travel since they were obligated to stay within the boundaries of their feudal lord.

Carts were a popular form of **medieval** transportation.

Political and religious travel

Despite the dangers, a number of people did travel. Kings had to travel on political campaigns and to conduct business. They had to visit powerful people to check on the kingdom and maintain a base of support for their rule. Religious leaders had to travel to promote their beliefs. And other people wanted to go on **pilgrimages** for religious reasons. In the Middle Ages, people traveled on foot, on the back of an animal such as a horse, or in a cart pulled by an animal.

People might travel great distances on religious pilgrimages. These pilgrims have arrived at the Church of the Holy Sepulchre in Jerusalem.

Trade and Exploration

Travel for trade

While most people did not travel much in the Middle Ages, curiosity about the world and a desire for foreign **trade** encouraged some explorers, such as Marco Polo and Christopher Columbus, to venture afar. The gradual development of navigational instruments, such as the magnetic compass, helped seafarers to find their way.

Local trade

Things such as spices and fabrics were the reward for those who ventured out to trade.

A new invention, the magnetic compass, allowed ship captains to steer more accurately. A magnetic compass has a pointer that indicates which direction is north, south, east, and west.

Trade took place across much of Europe during the Middle Ages.

Often trade was between nearby cities. Certain cities were known for their beautiful glass. Others were known for their jewelry or tapestries. Growing cities provided a place to meet and trade.

The wealthy had many options when purchasing goods.

Cities began to be known for the goods they produced. Cities in France were known for dyes. Venice was known for glass. Spanish cities were known for leather. Quality sugar came from Sicily. England produced wool. Fur was imported from Russia. Fish came in from Scandinavia. Regional trading systems formed around major cities. Agricultural goods brought to the city were traded for imported or manufactured goods.

As trade increased, so did the size and activity of cities.

Plague

People in the Middle Ages did not realize
that germs caused disease. Piles of garbage
lined the streets. The garbage attracted rats.
The rats carried fleas that could transmit a
disease called bubonic **plague.** In 1348 C.E.,
a plague struck Europe.

This plague was called the "Black Death"
because people who were sick with it got
black spots all over their bodies. Many people
have assumed that this "Black Death" was
bubonic plague. Millions of Europeans died
from plague. There is no way to know exactly

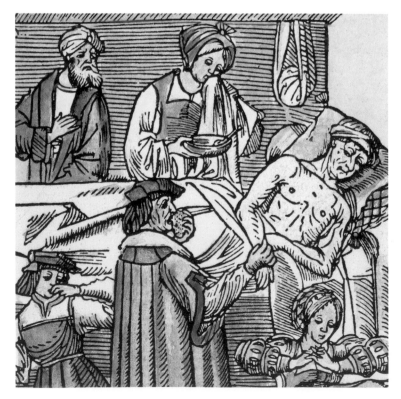

The Black Death was a
frightening disease. In
this picture, the doctor
and his helper are
holding perfumed cloths
to their noses to ward
off the smell of the
plague victim.

During the time of the plague, people buried bodies by the hundreds everyday.

how many people died from the plague or how long it lasted. It traveled through all of Europe, into Asia, and reached as far as Greenland.

Was it bubonic plague?

Historians are still studying what is known of this European plague in order to figure out if it really was bubonic plague. There are new theories about other diseases. One thing historians have realized is that there was no evidence of a lot of rats dying at the time. They normally would have gotten bubonic plague first. Also, the season was not the typical one for this disease to spread.

Warfare and the Decline of Feudalism

Warfare

War was frequent in the Middle Ages as land, politics, and religion were disputed. The **castle** was built to be a fortress that would offer safety and defense. Arrow slits allowed archers to shoot through the thin openings, while still being protected by the stone walls. The drawbridge was pulled up to prevent entry and dungeons secured any prisoners.

Stairs wound up the outside of the castle wall in a clockwise direction, making it difficult for right-handed attackers to swing their sword without being blocked by the side of the castle. A well in the castle provided water for drinking and putting out fires. Gunpowder was a new **medieval** weapon. It was used as an explosive to destroy castle walls, and for cannons.

There were many wars in the Middle Ages. Often, they were caused when one **lord** tried to take over the property of another.

In times of peace, a lord kept only a few soldiers to guard the castle and a handful of men-at-arms. For siege, a lord needed more knights. They fought with **maces,** swords, lances, and axes. **Nobles** hired professional soldiers, called mercenaries, to guard the castle. When under attack, people from the villages fled within the town walls. People brought all the belongings and animals they could. They set fire to their village so the enemy would not get what was left behind.

As the feudal system collapsed, a middle class emerged in western Europe.

Decline of feudalism

The **feudal system** could not last forever. It depended upon an economy based on farming. More people were becoming **merchants** and craftworkers. It was also a system that depended on peasants and **serfs.** Increasingly, peasants and serfs began to expect something different for their lives.

A drastic reduction in population due to **plague** also made it difficult to maintain the feudal system. There were not enough people to work the land. The remaining laborers were needed so much that they could ask for, and receive, different types of work and pay. **City-states** and **nations** began to emerge.

New Ideas

By the end of the Middle Ages, laws began to replace warfare and there was more peace in the land. This promoted **trade**. The **Renaissance,** a time of rebirth, had begun. Adventurers went on voyages of exploration. Lands unknown to western Europeans were discovered. The **medieval** invention of eyeglasses would lead to the Renaissance invention of the telescope, to give people a clear view of the sky. The invention of the telescope would later lead to the microscope, which solved some of the mystery of disease.

The optical lenses used for eyeglasses would later prove useful in creating telescopes and microscopes.

Art and books

The art of classic Greece and Rome was unearthed and enthusiastically imitated by artists such as Leonardo da Vinci and Michelangelo Buonarroti. People enjoyed new, affordable books that were inexpensively reproduced on the new invention, the **printing press.** More people learned to read and popular literature was everywhere. People studied a variety of subjects. A fascination with everything human sparked curiosity in the arts and sciences, and gave birth to invention and creativity.

The Middle Ages culminated in a time of artistic, literary, and philosophical "rebirth" known as the Renaissance.

What Remains

The Middle Ages were a time of war, **plague,** and famine. Many conflicts were addressed with brutal punishment.

A better life for serfs

In contrast, the Middle Ages were also a time when people developed notions of knightly courage, devotion, and romantic ideas. **Serfs** moved out of their dependency upon a feudal **lord** and a new middle class emerged in western Europe. People could hope for a better life and have a real chance of obtaining it.

The Middle Ages brought about a shift from a rural to an urban economy in western Europe.

Changes

The culmination of the conflicts of the Middle Ages was a period of creativity, invention, and new ideas. People turned to nature for beauty and happiness. They became fascinated with what it means to be human. Religion underwent many changes. Protestant religions emerged as did more appreciation for Judaism and Islam.

Life as a story

Today, the Middle Ages are a source of stories about people struggling to live their lives within very defined rules. Powerful royalty, wealthy **nobles**, loyal and courageous knights, enterprising **merchants**, creative artists and craftworkers, devoted and hardworking peasants, are characterized again and again in folktales and epics. The **medieval** stories of King Arthur and Merlin are still popular today. In studying their lives, we gain insight into our own.

The emergence of a middle class and a shift towards an urban, commercial economy in western Europe and elsewhere can be at least partially linked to events of the Middle Ages.

Time Line

476	The **Roman Empire** falls.
742	Charlemagne is born.
851	The crossbow is invented.
1000	Leif Eriksson lands on the North American coast.
1000s–1100s	The emergence of guilds.
1066	William the Conqueror invades England and asserts his right to the throne at the Battle of Hastings.
1067	Construction on the Tower of London begins.
1095	The First **Crusade** occurs.
1096	Peter the Hermit leads the Peasant's Crusade.
1100	The Virgin Mary is declared a saint in the Christian religion. She is the first woman to be so recognized.
1150	The Chinese develop rockets.
1165	The idea of **chivalry** emerges. Chivalry includes the defense of honor, combat in tournaments, and the virtues of generosity and reverence.
1170	The first European windmill is developed.
1180	Glass mirrors are first used.
1200	An increased number of people are receiving formal education.
1215	King John signs the Magna Carta.
1265	Dante, author of the *Divine Comedy*, is born. His work is considered some of the greatest of the Middle Ages.

1267 Florentine Giotto, the most important painter of the later Middle Ages, begins the modern tradition in painting.

1271–1295 Marco Polo travels to and around China.

1272 Edward I of England establishes Parliament, a feudal court for the king and not yet a system of representative government.

1280 Eyeglasses are invented.

1315 Bad weather and crop failure result in famine across northwestern Europe.

1330 The use of cannons in warfare begins.

c.1348–1349 Thousands of people die from **plague.**

1385 The first German university is opened in Heidelberg.

1387–90 Geoffrey Chaucer writes *The Canterbury Tales.*

1412 Joan of Arc is born.

1429 Joan of Arc leads a French revolt and is killed in England.

1440 Gutenberg invents the **printing press.**

1454 Italy is divided into five major regions: Venice, Milan, Florence, the Papal States, and the southern kingdoms of Naples.

1481 The Spanish Inquisition begins.

1492 Columbus sails across the Atlantic Ocean. King Ferdinand and Queen Isabella expel all Jews from Spain.

1517 The **Protestant Reformation.**

Glossary

acrobat person who is very good at stunts like jumping, balancing, tumbling, and swinging from things

alliance agreement between regions in which each promises to defend the interests of the other

apprentice young person learning the trade or skill of an expert

architecture art of making plans for buildings; style of a building

artisan person skilled in arts or craftwork

castle large, fortified home, often with a tower and other defensive features such as a drawbridge and moat

chivalry code of conduct for virtuous and charitable qualities in knights

city-state politically independent city

clergy ordained members of a church, such as priests, nuns, and monks

cloister covered walkway, passage, or room in a monastery

Constantinople modern-day Istanbul, Turkey

crusade military expedition made by Christian countries in the 11th, 12th, and 13th centuries to recover holy land from the Muslims and convert non-Christians

damask fancy cloth used especially for household linen

evangelist Christian preacher who goes from place to place trying to change or increase people's religious feelings

family lineage blood relatives and direct ancestors through which social class, titles, and status are inherited

fast to go without eating

fennel plant similar to parsley

feudal system system by which poorer people lived on richer people's land in exchange for some sort of service

flax plant from which linen is made

fresco style of painting whereby pictures are created on wet plaster and become a permanent part of the wall

gold leaf very thin, gold foil used to edge book pages or decorate letters and pictures on the pages

humor name given to bodily fluids that people in the Middle Ages believed were responsible for a person's health

hyssop plant similar to mint

lord person having power and authority over others

mace heavy war club with a spiked head

medieval having to do with the Middle Ages

melee hand-to-hand fight among several people

merchant person who buys goods in one place and sells them in another, often in a different country

midwife person who assists in childbirth, usually a woman

minstrel person who sings as entertainment

monk member of a religious group of men who live in monasteries away from the rest of the world

mosaic art in which small tiles or other small pieces are joined to form a design

nation country or group of people unified by a common government
noble person born into an important family; a man of noble rank was sometimes called a *nobleman*

ordain to enter into a religious vocation

patron person who financially supports an artist
pewter metal used for cups and other objects; was known as poor man's silver
pilgrimage journey to a holy place, often as an act of devotion
plague destructive, epidemic disease
printing press similar to a grape or olive press, in which inked templates are pressed onto paper to make books
Protestant Reformation movement to reform the Catholic Church, it led to a new branch of Christianity called Protestantism

Renaissance rebirth; used to name the period of cultural rebirth in Europe
retainer servant
Roman Empire lands and people under the rule of ancient Rome

seal small object with pictures or words used to make impressions
serf person who works on land overseen by a lord

tithe tax paid to a church
trade to buy and sell goods
Turk native of Turkey, person who speaks Turkish, or a person of Turkish descent

verjuice light dressing made with juice

wild boar wild pig

More Books to Read

Langley, Andrew. *Medieval Life.* New York: Dorling Kindersley, 2000.

MacDonald, Fiona. *Women in Medieval Times.* Columbus, Ohio: McGraw-Hill Children's Publishing, 2000.

Reid, Struan. *Marco Polo.* Chicago: Heinemann Library, 2001.

Steele, Phillip. *Medieval World.* New York: Houghton-Mifflin Company, 2000.

Index